From River to River

Thoughts on Life in the Great Bend

Writers on the Avenue

DEDICATION

flowing
like the waters
from river to river

joining
intertwining
becoming
more than possible

our words
are for you.

--Gesene Oak

CONTENTS

ACKNOWLEDGEMENTS

Salvatore Marici's poem "Summer Wane in Upper Mississippi Valley" appears in his book *Fermentations,* published by Ice Cube Press.

Dennis Maulsby's poem "Reflections" appears in his collection *Near Death/Near Life* (Prolific Press, 2015). "Paddy Morgan" first appeared in the 2008 edition of *Feile-Festa* and also appears in *Near Death/Dear Life.*

WINNERS
AND FAVORITES

from our 2018 poetry contest

Adult Category

RICHARD THURSTON

Summer

Arching green canopies
high overhead.
Cool shady comfort.
Leaves flutter gently
in hypnotic motion.
Cicadas singing
an endless song.

Spring

Tender branches
young and limber.
Buds half open
on the timber.
Dancing wildly
in the breeze.
A gentle rain
upon the trees.

Autumn

Kaleidoscopic color.
Swirling, drifting
falling down.
Orange, yellow
red and brown.
A mosaic carpet
on the ground.

Winter

Ice-caked trees
creak in gusts of wind.
Long bare branches reach upward.
Cold naked fingers
grasp at the warm sun.

Standing in the Forest

I stand in the forest
in winter, suffering
the wind and snow.

I stand in the forest
in spring, when buds
and leaves grow.

I stand in the forest
in summer, enduring
the rainless heat.

I stand in the forest
in autumn, dropping
nuts for the squirrels to eat.

I stand as a silent
sentinel, and witness
the passing of time.

I have recorded the ages
of history, within these
rings of mine.

Photo by Dustin Joy

2ᵈ PLACE WINNER:

RICHARD BIERMAN

Panorama

We chopper out of Uplift to find a lost patrol.
Shades of brilliant green and brown make a checkerboard below.

To the east I see the ocean and a ribbon of white sand,
And in the west the wooded hills of Montagnard land.

Villages and rice paddies upon the valley floor
Stretch from jungled mountains to the distant ocean shore.

There are no bands of asphalt, no noisy motor bikes.
The hamlets are connected by dusty trails and dikes.

Black pajamaed farmers are stooped in flooded beds.
They tend their rice with ancient tools, wearing straw cones on
their heads.

Children dart between grass huts a thousand feet below.
They play the same games children played a hundred years ago.

As we chopper from the valley, returning it to peace,
The mountains spread a welcome with their jungled canopies.

Rocky streams flow gently between their emerald walls,
Then burst out of the jungle in sparkling waterfalls.

The green hills rise around us with crowns of waving grass,
And trees spring from the shoulders of the stony cliffs we pass.

And now it's time to go to work, our saddle is in sight.
Our peaceful ride comes to an end as we prepare to fight.

Hard Eyes

Qui Nhon nurse stands by my side. I'm weary and hurt.
I stink of sweat and fever and a week of jungle dirt.

An emptiness burns in my soul, the days have been too long.
The fighting has been bloody and the mountains have been strong.

Qui Nhon nurse, you're young like me—why do you look so old?
What have we seen, so far from home, that made our hearts turn
cold?

You've never seen a killing zone, where friends cry out in pain.
But you've heard mine cry for loved ones they will never see again.

The sights of battle I have known, your eyes will never see.
But deep inside my heart, I know, you're just as tough as me.

So many people suffering, so many shattered lives;
The tears no longer come to us, they dry inside hard eyes.

Killer Team

Company C killer teams are stalking NVA.
But Charlie knows we're searching, so there's no contact today.

Our air assault is three days past, since then we've killed a few.
They died beside a weapons cache and they took Johnson, too.

The jungle trails are empty now, but NVA are near.
They know that we are hunting them, and so they disappear.

We break into a clearing far beneath a jungled crest.
Six choppers move in from the east, flying two abreast.

We hope that Charlie's watching, but we don't want him to see
That men lay flat on chopper floors, the men of Company B.

The choppers drop in two at once upon the sloping green.
We climb into the outside doors and jump out in between.

We lay low in the tall grass as the choppers fly away.
The Bravo troops sit in the doors, with luck our trap will pay.

We crawl down to the treeline and move out quietly.
It's time to wait by steaming trails beneath the canopy.

The NVA saw empty slicks takes GIs off the hill.
They fill their jungle highways then, and we begin to kill.

Artwork by Mike Fladlien

3^d PLACE WINNER:

MIKE FLADLIEN

Empty basket
Carries memories
Of past harvests

Mike Fladlien

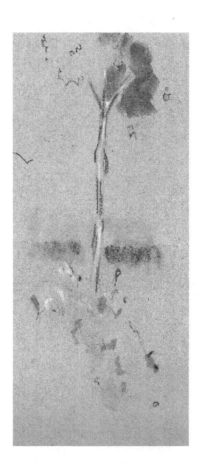

Gavel strikes.
Silence in the courtroom.
Sobbing

Mike Fladlien

She played the violin
Like it was her soul
Crying

Late Autumn

Rocking in her chair

Looking out her window

And over her life,

In her mind, she saw

       Children playing

       Awkward teenage years

       Marriage

And now a lonely house

It was late autumn

Arthritic leaves lay on the ground

Under a blanket of frost.

The days are shorter now.

       She is a mother again

       Then a teen

       Then an infant

Being rocked to sleep

HONORABLE MENTION:

VICKY DOVENSPIKE

And the Winner Is . . .

As hard as it tried
the bare tree could not stop the wind.
Empty arms outstretched to block,
but it could not.

Branches bouncing, jerking,
jumping and swaying,
diving high then low,
but the wind did not slow.

The wind just laughed
"I make the rules–
It's a game you can't win."
The tree bowed with a bend.

Dreams

I watch sun's colors melt into the horizon.
Breathtaking orange, red, and yellow
flow from the brush ... in this hand of mine.

My words travel like a rushing waterfall;
powerful, clear, continuous,
escaping from the pen ... in this hand of mine.

Waking in the night;
vivid, detailed, words and scenes,
endless inspiration ... fill this head of mine.

How can I make a living on these dreams of mine?

You and I

When I was lost
you found me

When I was alone
you stood by me

When I was afraid
you calmed me

When I was disillusioned
you freed me

When I was unsure
you waited for me

When I reached out
You were there

I Applaud

I was a captivated audience.
The performance was outstanding.
Voices rose one by one, louder and
louder for nearly twenty minutes
they sang, then slowly began to fade.
I was moved by the words I could
not understand, motivated by the
cheerfulness they spread in this
early hour.

Oh little song birds,
you ask for nothing
and give so much.

HONORABLE MENTION:

DAN MOORE

You Know It's Spring When

You can have a spring when lean robins don't sing.
    You can have one without cleaning.
You can miss daffodils, and the flowers' frills.
    Without baseball, it's demeaning.

The crack of the bat and the tilt of the cap
    Are harbingers of better times,
Both when snows don't fly and the black batter's eye
    Bring sounds of leather-smacking chimes.

Hey, batter batter, you know what's the matter.
    You can't hit a ball with a slide.
You can't stand the heat, you step back with your feet.
    The Mendoza Line's your high tide.

The pitcher winds up, shortstops adjust their cup,
    The fielder bends over to spit.
This lengthens the game, their nerves trying to tame.
    Women yelling, "Get on with it!"

The freshly cut grass feels good if you run fast
    For a quickly sinking line drive.
Teams with triple threats are as good as it gets;
    Then your pennant chances will thrive.

If you must dive to keep an inning alive,
    You'll be rewarded for your hustle.
On a bang-bang play, no matter what you say,
    It could end up in a tussle.

Black pine tar resin, pepper with your cousin,
    Are signs summer is almost here.
No need to remind us that peanuts bind us,
    Unless well-washed down with a beer.

Ketchup and mustard are a hot dog's custard.
    You just relish the very thought.
A team-signed baseball is the best gift of all,
    Since it did not have to be bought.

Put off your blanket; see the sun and thank it.
    Put up remote and down the pen.
You should go play outside, where their dugouts chide.
    'Cause you know that it's spring when.

Where You From?

Wherever you are from, whether bright or glum,
 The name to which we oft refer,
Once it's referenced, conversation can commence,
 And your heritage we infer.

Most national names play their simple word games
 Of adding something with a pen.
For Russians or Prussians or the Chadians,
 We simply add on I - A - N.

This creates a tag to put you in one bag
 With folks of your institution.
It's not very classy, some would say crassie;
 But it's a simple solution.

From Scotland are Scots, and they're unruly lots,
 A fact to which most Brits agree.
The Flemish aren't phlegmish, but Danes are Danish;
 East Indians are now Bengali.

There are good natured Thais, Hindus from Mumbai,
 And Ivorians from Côte D'Ivoire.
And any small clique from darkest Mozambique
 Does not play with the Quebecoise.

One night I dined and drank with a robust Franc,
 But I've not met a Yemeni.
Rode with an Uzbek and a man from Utrecht;
 Was marooned with an Omani.

Kazakhs are herders and the Luxemburgers
  Don't come with lettuce and stink cheese.
The Costa Ricans aren't Last of Mohicans,
  Neither are the nice Sudanese.

Limburgers are Dutch, wooden shoes and the such,
  Noted for cheese with aroma.
The Swiss, not the Poles, former's cheese filled with holes,
  Are guards in Vatican's Roma.

The somber Polish deal in amber and fish,
  Not aforementioned Helvetians.
Mongols use camels and Greeks have fine damsels,
  While Italians have Venetians.

Split identity gives dual indemnity,
  Such as the Flemish and Walloons.
Both are Belgian, though their families meld in,
  Not so with them of Cameroon.

Though close together, oft different is better,
  Like folks of Portugal and Spain.
Portuguese may wheeze with the lightest of breeze.
  Like Spaniards, they're Iberiaine.

Asia has Chinese, Africa Congolese,
  And Finnish are not Finnians.
Don't confuse Croatians or dark-skinned Haitians,
  With Serb-Hertzagovinians.

From Rome come Romans and not Romanians;
  The latter live on the Black Sea.
The Emerald Isle has Irish, Swedes are Swedish,
  And the Turks, of course, from Turkey.

At first confusing, for those who are using
  Terms for Turks and Caicos Islands.
Of course, they're not Turks, when in fact what there lurks
  Are Brits from the Scottish Highlands.

The worst name that I know refers to Glasgow,
  The poorly named Glaswegians.
Hungary has Magyars, west China has Uyghurs.
  South Pacific has Fijians.

The coolest-sounding, with syllables rounding,
  Tones that hit the ear not too hard,
Are folks from Savoy; every girl and boy
  There are known as the Savoyard.

Some vote for Parisian or for Venetian,
  And for those of the Argentines.
Second-best to hear, like a fresh-opened beer,
  Are the ones who are Florentine.

After the mighty Casey struck out at bat,
he found success as a Mudville poet.

JUDGE, ADULT CATEGORY:

DENNIS MAULSBY

Reflections

Reflections in the shaving mirror,
my body crouched in jungle fatigues,
blood splatter on my cheeks.
the rifle breach spins golden brass.

Reflections in river ice.
Under the bridge, in fusty ragged
uniforms, my comrades huddle
around a smoky barrel fire.

Reflections on the curved glass
of my intravenous bottle.
Drip, drip, drip.
Agent Orange seeks its level.

Reflections in my car hood's
flaking blue-pearl paint
of a speeding 18-wheeler bumper,
a gift of suicide by trucker.

Reflections in the sunglasses
of a fur-voiced priest.
The sound of gravel
rattles on my hollow coffin top.

Paddy Morgan

Me Ma and Da found a safe home
In Spoon River, fleein' from
The Famine. They bound me
Ta the wild songs o' Old Erin.
I became yer fiddlerman
An' called up the magic o' the dance.
Well now, ya hired me
When ya wanted yer spirits ta soar.
Me fiddle made yer feet flash--
All the lasses' petticoats spinnin' out
Like flowers bloomin', their petals
Blue, ivory, an' peach. Twists o' lilac,
Women's scent, drifted in the air,
Spun off golden skin by the dance's heat.
A bit o' poteen ta quench me thirst,
An' me bow work dazzled yer eyes.
Faster . . . faster--heel an' toe,
Polishin' the wood floor with yer soles,
An' yer souls with whoops o' joy.
Then came a day o' darkness an' silence.
Ya buried me with fiddle an' bow.
Jaysus, I wish I could play again. Aye!

Teen Category

BAILAH BOGNAR

She gazes onward
Envisioning a better world
A hope of change and peace
A breeze flies past
Reality coming with it
She watches the setting sun
Remembering wise words
Only change can come with hope
And hope with courage
She turns away and walks back into the darkness
Knowing things must happen to bring
The light back into her world
A world that was filled with broken things
Needing to be fixed and renewed
She would not fear what lies ahead
Nor would she be cut by the pieces of the shattered land
She knew there were others like her
Believers, dreamers, fighters
She'd find them, all of them
And together they'd shine through the dark
Ride the world of demise and deceit
Then build a better world and make a dream into reality

HONORABLE MENTION:

MADISON HEISCH

A Love for the Game

An echo of the ball hitting the hardwood
And the obsessive sound of the snap of the net
The want and the need for the game
A feeling in your hands that nothing can replace
Even the drained feeling when you are done
The feeling of success is great,
But defeat is a bitter blow
Although games will be won and lost,
The season is never over.

Youth Category

1ST PLACE WINNER:

KEVIN CISS

Thanksgiving

I. The first thing I am grateful for is my great family all around the world. I love all my relatives and I enjoy seeing how they live their lives. They are all different, but we all believe in God, and I love Thanksgiving because it brings us closer together.

II. The second thing I am grateful for is my school. I love making new friends with people I never knew and learning about them. I also like learning new things, praying at mass, and all the teachers are nice. I feel lucky to go to SMMCS.

III. The third thing I am grateful for is the Mississippi. I love watching the deep blue crests of the river from up on the rock. When I stand on the edge of the water, I imagine that Jesus and my grandpa are bobbing in the water and we are watching the sky.

IV. The fourth thing I am grateful for is my parents. My mom always helps me with my homework and she is always near. My dad has always helped me accomplish my dreams, both big and small. I love looking at them and seeing the Holy Spirit in them.

V. The fifth thing I am grateful for is the sky. I love to look at the clouds and watch them move and spin. Sometimes I dream that a stairway of light descends and I walk up it into heaven. The stars remind me of the Old Testament. At first there was one star, just like there was one human. But God allowed us to multiply and thrive on earth.

VI. The sixth thing I am thankful for is the animals. I always walk through the woods on summer days. Sometimes I watch the squirrels scurry across the branches and eat acorns. When I get the chance, I take my kite out into the field and watch the ladybugs fly and the red tailed hawks soar. I love that God took the time to create these furry friends of the wild.

VII. The seventh thing I am thankful for is the plants. I love spruce trees and the texture of birch trees is amazing. I pick berries by the river in fall with my mom, and I ride my scooter under the archway of bushes and mulberry trees. It all reminds me of the Garden of Eden.

VIII. The eighth thing I am grateful for is food. The only thing I won't eat is eggs. I love chewing food and I love cooking even more than I love eating. Whenever my mom and I celebrate, we make homemade pie. My mom's gift from God is to bake.

IX. The ninth thing I am grateful for is mystery. When I look for something I feel depressed, but when I find it, I feel proud. I love waiting to see where we are going for Christmas and I love the thrill of solving mysteries.

X. The last thing I am grateful for is free will. I know our actions caused pain and misery but I love not knowing what I will do next. I want to make my choices count and make the world better through my actions.

2^D PLACE WINNER:

CLIO VOGEL

The Month Poem

Playing in Summer Heat

pool

hot   fun

swimming   splashing   jumping

cool   smooth

us

August Rain

squiggly slippery

stomping   falling   surprising

drippy   wet

earth

Skiing

snow

soft   cold

rolling   flying   freezing

white   sparkly

lift

JUDGE, TEEN & YOUTH CATEGORIES:

DENISE SMITH

Stages of Life

Created by God
Born into the world
Depending on others
Learning basics
Learning rules
Learning boundaries
Learning about God
Making friends
Pursuing interests
Planning the future
Finding purpose
Finding a mate
Raising a family
Seeking God
Learning sacrifice
Learning patience
Managing time
Maintaining friendships
Establishing traditions
Gaining wisdom
Speaking to and of God
Experiencing empty nest
Renewing friendships
Making new friends
Finding purpose after retirement
Caring for elders
Loving grandchildren
Sharing memories

Accepting with humility
Losing loved ones
Keeping traditions
Slowing down
Looking back
Praising God
Enduring pain
Depending on others
Letting go
Returning to God.

We're passing through; remember what's important.

Poetry

Reading poetry isn't for everyone.
Some think it's a dying art, a penalty to read,
confusing, boring or too deep.

But if you look for the author's
thoughts, ideals and personality,
they become intimate details; fully opened truths.

Poetry is the shorthand of a fully written speech;
a kaleidoscope of words from the heart and mind.
I want to conserve the art by writing it.

Painting by Denise Smith

The Painting

I was painting and began to feel ageless,
drawn into the picture.
It was no typical place but ethereal,
with trees and moss, light and shadows,
foliage and a whispering breeze.
A path wove between trees
leading to an unknown future.
Night descends, casting shadows.
Amber light caresses the trees,
soothing the eyes.
I look at the canvas
and know I am finished.
The painting looked like it felt to be there.

Photo by Dustin Joy

WHAT WE KNOW

MIKE BAYLES

Blue Moon, Full Moon, Full Lunar Eclipse

The full-bodied moon
comes again this month
when she hides in earth shadows
from the sun.
I look at her faceless stare,
and she gazes through black skies at me.
Street lights of a slumbering town
on a hillside twinkle
while I drive alone
easing my way along
a winding road
and a gentle ballad plays
on the radio.
In a slow dance with the sun
she moves tides and seas
and tells stories of the universe.
Star light, a dream
blue moon, a wish
for a loved one to come back
when we'd embrace
and dance under endless skies.

Seen and Unseen

A broad spread of grassy hills
rolls beyond a small town.
A lone farmer tends to a land
far beyond the prairies I know.
His children move
to distant cities and towns.
Beyond hills and twists in the road
lies a reservation
where Native Americans
reclaim the land.
Far beyond a wind cave breathes,
its intricate formations carved
by water dripping underground
discovered when an explorer felt
the breath of life's source.
The Lakota say all life
lived in this cavern
when the earth above was formed.
The proud sun to the west
casts light on an ancient land
eager to tell stories
lying in folds of the land.
I lose track of time
on the long journey home
embracing images of a timeless place
to be held within chambers of my heart.

Driftwood on Shore

water lapping at your feet
a castoff cast
on the ragged shoreline
a bend in the river
a cloud in the sky
sunlight reflections on waves
a sign on a path
marking 10,000 steps
stories told
upriver music plays
for anyone who will dance
wind sweeping across water
unspoken conversations
about life and death
driftwood on shore

Photo by Dustin Joy

ALAN ARKEMA

The Lane

I trod a tree-lined lane today
Where sun-crusted snow lay
In patches. Rivulets frozen deep
In ancient ruts up the steep
Hillside warned my feet beware:
"Feet poorly shod will not fare well here."

When springtime thaw exiles snow and frost
I'll trod the lane at greater cost.
The clinging soil
Make heavy feet and greater toil.
But spring will yield to summer climes.
I'll trod this lane in freer times.

When lovers trod a lane together,
Life is easier in any weather.
Feet fall more safely when
They're brac'd by a friend.
So come and walk through life with me.
We'll trod this lane together.

Our love will brace and comfort be
When comes the stormy weather.
'Twill also help us joy the sun
Or sandy beach in summer fun.
Our feet will fall more safely when
We keep love alive until the end.

To a 'Valentine'

Your soft brown eyes look deep
Into the soul of me, I fear,
Noting every fault and weakness there.
Yet your friendship's given free.

I bare my inner soul to you,
Crying out in agony and pain.
Answ'ring hug: a soft refreshing rain.
Gentle caress: the rose's morning dew.

Your soft brown eyes have come
To bless me recently, I know,
Soothing away the pain of long ago.
I'm at peace in my new home.

I'd not paint you perfect—'tis unfair.
The gift you have you've given me:
Your kindness from a heart so free.
Such love's a treasure rare.

DUSTIN JOY

In Elmira

In Elmira there's a place up on a hill.
It lies near the summit but not quite.
A place of silence now which never will
host the raspy voice of the man in white.

His stone is nothing special and no larger
than many others under oaks there spread.
Indeed within this plot he is a lodger;
the yard below contains his in-laws' dead.

And that is no surprise to those who love him.
He never had one place which was his own.
Hannibal and Hartford both may claim him,
but *An Innocent Abroad* must always roam.

About him lie his own dear departed,
his treasures taken from him premature.
Tragedies profound that once they started
took his faith and gave him illness with no cure.

From the Cairo that lies on the Mississippi,
to the one nearby the mighty flowing Nile,
He was known and praised and loved by millions
and there were fortunes heaped around him in a pile.

All men knew about the famous Yankee
and the adventures of Huck n' Tom n' Jim,
the jumping frog of Calaveras County,
his examination of old Adam's sin.

Sometimes it seems he soured on the people,
the very ones who made of him a star.
And even when he chastened them they loved it;
Hadleyburgers cannot see just who they are.

But he must have seen in them a thing worth saving,
Lest why the moral lesson hid within.
"All right I'll go to Hell" was not just raving;
it saved the soul of Huckleberry Finn.

And when the sad and lonely days persisted,
and when he'd turned his back against his God,
even though *The Mysterious Stranger* insisted
that we are all just bugs on which he trod,

but though Sam gave up on religion,
and ultimately gave up on his own life,
he left us all a treasure of his vision
that perhaps the world need not end in strife.

For though we all be Pudd'nheads and greedy,
selfish, foolish purveyors of shame,
though gods and angels do not help the needy,
we poor humans do not deserve the blame.

We did not make the world and what is in it.
Mr. Clemens has absolved us of our sins.
All that we can do is to do better.
A better code was offered up by him.

A tiny little lie is not important.
Imbibing and partaking minor sins.
Sometimes what matters isn't what is spoken,
but those sentiments not heard above the din.

Every man has dignity and purpose
Whether he be fancy or be plain.
Kings and Congressmen, it's all a circus.
All of them were but as one to Twain.

All are to be in some ways respected;
All are to be ridiculed and shamed.
Not because of how they were pigmented,
But because we shared that apple all the same.

Now his bones lie high above this river.
His tormented days on earth are done.
He blazed across our world like Haley's Comet,
And to us his words still offer up the sun.

Dustin Joy and Mark Twain

JUDY HASKINS

Indigo Mood

You think you have anonymity, but I know who you are.
You sneak into my life to steal my happiness, life as I know it.
When you're here, I'm befuddled, unable to concentrate,
Make simple decisions, enjoy the things I used to.
Discontent mushrooms into indigo mood.
Soon, like a popinjay, you demand all my attention.
Interned by your robust attack on my psyche,
I'm an overturned kayak on the lake.
I cannot swim. I cannot breathe.
I've been here before and will be again.

To be rid of you is a chimera.
To acknowledge and feel you allows forward movement.
I'll take back my life by cultivating gratitude and love
As I journey through the kaleidoscope of emotion
To confidence, clear thinking and joy.

Water falls
Creates rainbows
Crashes on boulders
Trickles over stones

JUDY CHAPMAN

Forgotten Memories

Remembrances clamor, but remain nebulous as sea foam,
Never coalescing to sharp detail though I try time after time.
Past images vigorously strive to become the present,
And long-forgotten memories suddenly cascade into
consciousness.

Church bells chiming the hour at sunset, wind rustling
through ordered rows of corn on a warm summer night.
Twain's Mississippi changing frocks with each passing season.
Recollections of their beauty pierce my soul with exquisite pain.

A treasured Christmas and a birthday cake baked long ago,
Beloved memories of parents forever young,
Early morning walks to school, seeing each tiny twig coldly aflame,
The bright sun twinkling on its blanket of ice.

Nights spent half-buried in Grandma's soft, deep feather bed
Listening to the incessant tick, ticking of the mantel clock.
Granddad slowly sliding knife blades across coarse whetstone,
Readying them for the next day's catch.

Too many thoughts battle for attention, seeming sharp yet hazy
with the ravages of time.
The reflections wound my soul, ruthlessly draining me,
Yet too sweet to allow them to pass into oblivion.
But, alas, they are moments forever lost, never to be regained.

A June Day

It's here: the long-awaited spectacle of June.
Nature has been preparing her incredible feast for months,
And now the greatly anticipated time has come.
Open for viewing are all of her magnificent wonders to behold.

There's no time that I enjoy driving more than the month of June.
There is no place that I enjoy driving more than in the Midwest.
There are more colors of green to be seen in one square mile.
There is more golden sunshine over emerald green fields.

Neighboring houses, washed spotless by spring rains,
Display their shrubbery and bushes around spreading decks.
Flowers abound and vegetable gardens grow, promising delights,
Surrounded by large spacious lawns completing the masterpiece.

Overlooking are magnificent trees with their newly grown crowns.
So many varieties, so many sizes, no two alike, forming a haven.
The trees cover the streets, hills and valleys
Providing a comforting shade in the hot summer sun.

My favorite place to drive is the Iowa countryside
With its rolling hills, fertile black earth and fields of young corn.
Early evening, the golden sun shines on the black earth
And lazy sunbeams hover in the air through puffy white clouds.

This is my favorite time of day to drive and I can remember:
My dad would take the family out for early evening drives like this.
Missing: the sound of tires on the brick roads of Eighth Street.
Could this be one of the reasons I like to drive in Iowa in June?

YASMINE CRUZ

What We Value In Life

As I sit here, pondering life, time stops
As the million dollar question comes to me,
What is Life? What is my idea of Life?
My idea is that Life is everything we value,
Family, friends, love, our passions, our faith
Whatever we value is our own meaning of life.
The friends we've made, even those forgotten
Enjoying the time we spend with them,
Making them laugh and seeing them happy,
Feeling like we found our place in the world
And never feeling alone, even if they aren't there.
From close friends come brothers and sisters,
To us, they are family by everything but blood
Always there to support us through our struggles,
Though the obstacles of life shaped us into who we are now.
With our entire family supporting us through life,
We take this time to find what our passion is in life
Whether it be music that can be represented in magical ways
Or running a business, climbing the ranks to support a family.
Being confident in ourselves to pursue our dream in life,
We shall never forget our reasons to keep moving in life.
Even when everything is looking down and nothing goes
right
What we value in life motivates us to continue on,
To find our dream life with all that we value.

Yasmine Cruz

Humanity by Anonymous

What have we come to
A land not always free
Turning away those who come
Who come looking for freedom
What is so different about them
America,
Land of the free and home of the brave
Discriminating those of different countries
Different race, culture, religion, genders
Just being different makes us shun them
Refusing to give them the freedom we have
But aren't we all different, no one exactly the same
And we are all one race, the human race
No matter how different we may appear
On earth we are the same species here
Who have lost the ability to love one another
So believe in humanity
For if not, then we are not human
And by taking the time to find humanity
We are now taking full responsibility.

My Music

How can you see into my eyes
Living in my own world
No one knows who we are there
Perfect by nature, icons of
Self-indulgence
I found a grave, felt your life
You know, you're not the only one
I've been believing in something
So distant
It's true, we're all a little insane
Make me whole again, open your eyes
You don't remember me
But I remember you
Out on your own, cold and alone again
As many times as I wanted to
Tell you the truth
There's nothing that can change
The way I feel
Feed the fire till my soul
Breaks free
I can't run anymore,
I fall before you,
Nothing left
All that I am,
Broken, lifeless.

Photo by Dustin Joy

G. LOUIS HEATH

Spring Day

The people in my town are seeing dust for the first time
This year, as dirty piles of snow melt to release once-frozen

Particles. Newly risen crocuses, lawns, and residents stir in
Earnest after long winter. They walk the pathway along the

River, watch ice vanish as barges loaded with America's bounty
Resume traffic from the heartland. Dust glints in the light of longer

Days, giving a lazy feel to this vernal time our bones ached for,
Racked on hibernal La-Z-Boys, eyes doped on video games,

Souls captive to Facebook. This the modern scurvy riddance time,
My town's spring. In olden days, we foraged for dandelions and

Wild radish to quell our ails. Now we pry ourselves from chairs,
Our eyes from pixeled screens, to look for ways to dose our souls.

Photo by Pat Bieber

SALVATORE MARICI

Summer Wane in Upper Mississippi Valley

In a sky,
          day paints Egyptian blue
          an angel fluffs wings
whose breath wafts dry warmth
with specks of coolness.
Pockets of fading-green
spot crowns of trees like bubbles
above cartoon characters
filled with scripts
of leaves' last wishes.
Fallen apples, pears
ooze hard cider, bees slurp.
They brawl in sugared air.
Goldenrod spikes burst
metallic-yellow. Sun scatters lusters
some settle, some suspend.
Pumpkins, butternut squashes,
lie amidst seared vines, split tomatoes.

Then dusk,
a minute before yesterday,
owls' ears trace moles' scurries
who through small eyes
see sunlight dim.

Sunday Confessions on Maquoketa River

Like the capsule
where John Glenn sat
when shot into space
each person
usually four
capsulate themselves
in their kayaks.

In separate spaces
each floats downstream.
Waving leaves on banks
catch our attention. We hear
male tree frogs chant chirping clicks.

Then one of us dips his paddle,
keeps it straight
slows the craft, waits
or pulls water add speed
to currents' flow
until friends unite.

As bubbles in beer gulps
fizz throats,
thirst-residues slide
we talk thoughts
because kayaks won't leak
what they hear.

RICH HANSON

Salt

Lot's wife disobeyed
A command of God.
She looked back.
Most likely yearning
For a final glimpse of her home,
The land that held her parents' bones,
The land where she fell in love,
Where her children were born.
Her refuge
Her nest
Her garden of memories.

She was turned into salt
A pillar of hardened crystals,
Like the sleep in one's eye
Multiplied from mote to monolith.

How cruel of God to punish one
Simply for choosing to look back
Upon one's roots, home and nest;
The past that made us all what we are.

Don't look back!
How can we help but do so?
To deny our history
Is to deny ourselves.

A sailor asks his messmate
To "pass Lot's wife"
As though she's a whore
Hauled up a hawser
To be hidden below deck

To be shared among them.
An old salt's spice of life
Perhaps worth one's salt.

Yeah, pass Lot's wife.
That shaker laden
With tears of regret
Tears of longing
Tears of lamentation
Tears of frustration
Tears of despair,
and rarely, too rarely
Tears of joy.

Any man worth his salt
Knows that the salt of the Earth
Is derived from tears.

Rules of the Road

Pick your time wisely.
Make sure your feet are healthy,
Your legs and heart strong,
Your soul honed for hardship.
Pack a knife, water, pepper, some biscuits.
Leave the morning of a holiday.
That puts more miles behind you
Before they notice you're gone.

The star that glows on the bright end
Of the ladle we call The Little Dipper
Is Polaris, the North Star.
The Lord has set it there as a beacon.
Let it lead you to freedom.
Need guidance in daytime?
If you're heading north as you ought,
At morning your shadow's to your left.
It shifts to your right
During the hot afternoon sun.
No sun? Moss grows on the north side
Of a tree. Keep moving that direction.

Near the Mississippi?
Old Man River flows south,
Keep travelling against the current.
If you reach the Rock River
You can follow it toward Wisconsin.

Travel at night. Lay low during the day.
Darkness is your friend, your cloak,
Your concealment,
As is a thick morning fog.

Don't steal. Light no fire.
Do nothing to call attention to yourself.
Keep on looking back, over your shoulder.

You can't outrun dogs, but you can try
To outsmart them.
Wade in streams where your scent won't linger,
But for goodness sake be mindful of snakes.
Rub your feet with pepper, turpentine,
Even wild onions if you can find them,
Anything that will confound a hound's nose.
If you find an old cemetery, some say
That the dust of the dead, stirred into paste,
Gives off a smell that no dog dare follow.
Worse comes to worst you can use your knife
To gut a stubborn hound if one hunts you out.

Tall prairie grass makes good hiding,
But know what poison ivy and oak look like.
Taking a nap in either can lead to pain
Searing as that of an overseer's lash.
Fill up on water whether you're thirsty or not,
'Cause there's sure to come a time when you will be.
Keep on looking back, over your shoulder.

Godspeed on your journey, brave fugitive.
May courage, wisdom, luck
and the assistance of the Divine Savior
Lead you to good people, safe havens
And despite much hardship… to *Freedom.*

RALPH MONTRONE

A Fall Gem

It had been
    a clear warm day
    not overly so, and not humid—
    the kind of day a sensible man dies for,
    the sort fall gives us
    as a matter of course.
He opened the car door
    while he waited for his wife.
    the cool of an autumn eve
    had already begun to arrive,
    draping its cool caress about the shoulders
    of the bluffs along the Mississippi River.
It would rain tonight
    and then cool off tomorrow.
He couldn't wait
    for the next fall gem
    to come his way
    if fall had any more to give.

"Royalty" by Pat Bieber

GESENE OAK

below the dam
ice floes on black water
bald eagles hunt

To a Red-Winged Blackbird

You sing for me
(but not *to* me)
from the highest branch
of the river birch
beside the pond

I pause mid-jog
and stretch
watching your wings lift
against the spring blue sky
your bright red wing patches
flashing in the sun

As you put your entire self
into the sweetness
of your call
I wish
I could paint
your song
forever

A Moment Forever

her mind is empty

windswept clean

eighty-six years of living

abandoned without

regret

remorse no longer

bites

sorrow no longer

tears

in the pleasantry of

here and now

she rocks

still she rocks

Cuing June

ducklings puddle play
cool breeze sweeps
storm clouds away
fallen tree weeps sap

beneath cobwebbed eaves
robins' nest of twig and twine
houses broken eggs

giggles chase after
flickers in deepest shadows
fireflies escape hand

ESPERANCE CISS

A Mother's Creed

I believed in the power of dreams,
worked, walked, to find the dream,
shrugged off obstacles along the way
longed to see happiness come my way
I fainted my pain to show joy
I used my words for decoy
        shame, rejection and failure
          hidden with a veil from a tailor

After all these, time came to a still
Dreams crushed like grain in a mill

Here you come, with love and kiss
heart and soul showered with bliss
Your eyes, a light for me to see
The beauty in a world to be—
Little fingers, so soft, so delicate
they touch, calm, heal—
I appreciate,
        For HOPE keeps us alive
        LOVE is----------a solution
        GOD is---------redemption!

Photo by Dustin Joy

MIKE LERETTE

No More Handshakes

Enter the arena above and below,
spectators await the event

An old space with hard seats
and history lingering

The gladiators assume their roles
Whispered voices, then the silence

The beginning, dull. Protocol must
be followed before the thrill

A fat man in a bright red suit
Jolly, maybe. Mischievous, more.

An outburst, then the action has begun
The expected tilt in motion

Tit-for-tat, back and forth
Council holds their session

"If you were really a lovebird, you'd write me some poetry."

RICHARD ALLEN

21 Days

Well it's that time, 21 days is done
Believe me it's been serious
However, I've had fun.

I've seen friends come and I've
seen them go, yet I couldn't allow
that to change my flow.

My groove's on point, I'm
Keeping it smooth. I've learned
How to speak to people without
Being rude.

I'm beginning to get a grasp
On this recovery thang. What's
Cool is I can be myself and
Sometimes we slang. For those
Of you that don't know what
That means, slang is Ebonics from
A "Why B Normal" dope fiend.

Enough of that, let's keep it real,
Let me tell you how I really
Feel.

The day has begun, into the
Distance we see, nothing really
Because it's still a mystery

Richard Allen

The sun may shine, the snow
May stick. Reach out to someone
Today, for there are many who
Are still sick.

Just as we are, yet we must give
It away, the message of AA to
Brighten not only ours, but
Someone else's day.

So be inspirational and from
Thine heart stay true. Just for
Today stay Honest, Willing and
Open-Minded, too.

I Am

I am! the enemy of self.
The evil is within my mind
Devouring my cells replaced with lies.
Painful memories erase the pleasures I shared.

I Am! the Grim Reaper walking in my shadow.
Blossom of the devil's petals.

I Am! the stench
I Am! the shackled, molded in metal's heat.
I Am! like blown glass.
I Am! uniquely designed.

I Am! perfect in the womb of creation.
I Am! life's child scraped and scarred.
I Am! life's child placed on a pedestal
I Am! surrounded by foes.
I Am! love's grasp loosened by
dysfunctional bliss.

I Am! growth within a spiritual fog.
I Am! strength of a spider's web united.
I Am! courage upon the lion's mane.
I Am! fear covered with inner peace.
I Am! happiness wrapped in joy's light.

I Am! lust intertwined with love's passion.
I Am! past, I Am! future, I Am! today, I Am! then,
I Am! what was, I Am! now, I Am.

Photo by Pat Bieber

MISTY URBAN

Passage

The curtain in the window may be yellow, or blue;
the pattern turns inward.
In the next window, a green sign, "Cardoza." Family name?
Famous baseball player? A solemn
declaration of remembrance, like "remember the Alamo?"
The belfry atop city hall has no windows. See
the twisted metal stairs, the wide skirt of the bell,
the juddering rail at which the tourists stand, watching
the swelling river. And the belfry tower of the church,
      closed, black-shuttered.

The river flows onward, onward. Cars pass on the street. The
sound of traffic, dry leaves skipping pavement,
the quiet conversation of birds. There are five
more white antennae in the part of my hair
      and Lyle has lung cancer, stage four. Time
will never move backward. Pull the curtain,
if you have one. Look out. Throw your window
sash wide to the world and let it come in. Now,
before the river takes it.

Because this river will flood again, devouring
everything before it: hands of water
ripping open the black shutters, ringing
bells like the drowned city of Ys.
The holy curtain torn down, revealing the hidden;

Clock tower falling, smashing time,
pulling civilization under the roaring
fury of the flood. And somewhere
on the shoulders of the waters, Cardoza
rolling and nodding, winking at the sky.
Remember Lyle.
     Remember me.
          Remember we once were here.

The Me I Used to Be

The me I used to be
  was afraid of so much
  illness scorn shapes
  in the dark   of never
  being loved of never
  being important   of
  spiders snakes pretty
  people of letting go &
  not   being perfect
The me I used to be
  had good knees   bruised easily
  ran miles   healed slowly
  drove with hands at 2 and 10 o'
  clock   wore a watch balanced
  her checkbook knew the answers
  got good grades followed the rules
  colored inside the lines   dropped
  and lost   and broke things   keys
  purses ketchup bottles Corelle ware
  could stay awake all night talking
  about anything our lives the world
  the perplexities of our mother
When you left   I became   someone
  you wouldn't   recognize someone
   who drank   too much   boarded
 planes   with a credit card   and one bag
  swore   fell   screwed up   held grudges
 held too tightly   tried too hard threw my heart
    at the same closed doors   again   & again   & again

When the dew falls   for the last time   & the stars
   bloom & fade   and matter returns   to energy
I will   find you   and we will race
through the universe   twinned sparks
wave   then particle wave once more
    as we used to be
      fearless
        together
            again.

The Invisible Orange

The missed moments:

The face turned from another's tears   (unprofessional)
The kind word not said   (none of my business)
The guy in overalls holding a cardboard sign
        on the side of the road, or the car
In the ditch I didn't stop for because
        my car was full, because I was alone, because
        I was late, because it was bad weather, because I
        had my kids, because the car was empty
The people I let bully me   (I might have deserved it)
The bullies I didn't stand up to.

Because I am just. Because I am right. Because
I know better. Because I know best. Because I
am the teacher. Because I am the mom.
Because mine is the wrath of the righteous.

What is the thing that should be there?

The open hand. The soft palm. The Kleenex.
The yield, the flex, the branch bending
with sap, the humble wind, the serenity. The world
that turns always to the good, to the light. The hand
of a benevolent God. The stem, the root, the breath
that cleanses.   Plenitude.   Beatitude.
                Softness.   Softness.   Softness.
The dimpled curve, the rind, the shell,
    the pulp and flesh that make it an orange,
Without which   it is only water.

Picture by Rebecca Whitmore

REBECCA WHITMORE

Homeless in the City of Pearls

He sits dormant, rigid,
Veiled in the murky shadows,
Fixated on this night's performance
Of ever-changing hues.
The illuminated bridge the headliner,
Constellations and fireflies supporting cast.

In the secluded vault of his mind,
He composes melodies
To mate with the harmonizing lights.
A sensual ballad of longing
For humanity's embrace
Of love and acceptance.

He marks time
By the wax and wane of the moon
Blurred by ripples of tireless currents.
River passing without a glance his way,
Nor offer to carry him to the promised land
Away from this city of pearls.

Pausing to listen,
Unsure if he heard sounds
Or the incessant ramblings in his head,
He melts deeper into the darkness,
Cloaked in obscurity,
To become invisible in the light of day.

Photo by Dustin Joy

ANNA COUNTER

The River

It births on stage from deep below;
tinkling, sprinkling, sunlight twinkling.
Not knowing where its path will go;
splattering, clattering, careless chattering.

Forming its bed with child-like glee;
glowing, flowing, ever growing.
Exult, create, grow wild, run free;
slipping, skipping, onward tripping.

Down one hill, bend 'round another;
folding, scolding, always molding.
Gaining strength, joined by a brother;
meeting, greeting, one soul fleeting.

'Round the hill, head back, and then
tumbling, mumbling, low-voiced grumbling,
rejoin itself to race again;
pouring, roaring, white foam soaring.

It dares the rocks and finds its way;
roiling, toiling, deep pools boiling.
Creating rainbows with its spray;
smashing, crashing, onward dashing.

Progressing on, its life's blood sends;
whirling, swirling, eddies curling.
And when, at last the journey ends;
testing, resting, no more questing.

Quiet and deep, it joins the sea;
wending, spending, new life blending.
Claiming its place in eternity;
assessing, caressing, ever blessing.

And the sea is all.

ABOUT THE AUTHORS

Robert Allen is a golf course maintenance employee for the City of Muscatine, where he lives with his big blended family. His poems in this volume are about fighting his demons and being in recovery.

Alan Arkema calls Iowa his home state, though he spent his career as a clergyman in various states as well as five years in Australia. Lately his hobbies include writing short stories and novels. He's glad that life in Muscatine offers so many cultural advantages, such as the Art Center and Writers on the Avenue.

Mike Bayles has published poetry in several venues and in the books *Threshold, The Harbor I Seek,* and *The Rabbit House.* His book of literary collage, *Breakfast at the Good Hope Home,* was published by 918Studio Press and another book of poetry is forthcoming.

Pat Bieber enjoys studying how to improve her writing skills and sharing what she learns with others. She also enjoys writing poetry and is currently working on a novel. Her poems have been regularly selected for inclusion in *Lyrical Iowa.* Bieber writes under the name Gesene Oak.

Rick Bierman is a lifelong resident of Muscatine. He is married to Pam and they have three children and eight grandchildren. He graduated from Muscatine High School in 1967 and enlisted in the United States Army in February 1968. His poems describe his combat experiences with the Headhunter Platoon of Charlie Company, 1st Battalion of the 173rd Airborne Brigade.

Bailah Bognar is a teenage girl who loves to read, write, and hang out with friends. She has done intense ballet and studied art and has a deep passion for expressing herself creatively.

Judy Chapman was raised in Muscatine and lived in California for 25 years before returning. She runs a piano studio from her home. She began writing as a journalist and for the last 20 years has switched to prose and essays. She has been a member of Writers on the Avenue since 1993.

Esperance Ciss holds a Bilingual Degree from the University of Yaounde in Cameroon and a Nursing Degree from Black Hawk College in Moline, Illinois. She enjoys learning about the City of Pearls as she follows her two energetic kids, Pearly and Kevin, on playgrounds, school, woods and trails along the Mississippi River. Her guilty pleasure is being transported in few seconds of reverie, indulging the wonders of nature as she watches the sunset from her balcony with Pearly. Writing is one way she connects with her family, friends and the world.

At 11 years old, Kevin Ciss is a curious mind with a great ability to engage the world and nature around him through his writing. As an emergent writer, some of his poems— "Fluid Time" and "Seasons"—have been acknowledged in contests in the community.

Anna Counter is 81 and, after retiring, finally indulged her interest in writing. She has published two books with another in progress and three children's books in various stages of completion, along with poetry on subjects that hold her interest. "The River" was written to represent the human life journey from birth to death.

Yasmine Cruz is a young poet who wants to share her writing with the world. A student at MCC, she enjoys spending hours in the library in between classes and submitting her poems to the MCC newspaper, the *Calumet*. She plans to major in journalism but when not writing, you can find her in the kitchen, baking. She hopes to one day have her poems known worldwide.

Vicky Dovenspike has lived in Iowa most of her life. She has been published in *Lyrical Iowa* and her photograph was selected for the cover in 2015. She has published one book, *Sorrow To Sunshine*. She enjoys painting pet portraits, photography, writing poetry and traveling to visit her three grown children and two granddaughters. She may be reached at theartofbeingvicky@yahoo.com.

Mike Fladlien is a retired business teacher at Muscatine High School. He was recently inducted to the mock trial hall of fame. He loves his wife, Kathy, so much that she is his haiku.

Rich Hanson and his wife, Nancy, have lived in Monmouth, IL, for the past 30 years. He worked as a Supervisory Consumer Safety Inspector for the USDA until retiring in 2017. He has self-published one book of poetry and has been published in a number of publications, including the *North American Review*, where he was a finalist for the James Hearst Poetry Prize. He has also been nominated for a Pushcart Award. He's looking for a home for a novel and a volume of short stories at present, and has blogs linking to his poetry, short stories and Civil War articles.

Judy Haskins has lived in the Muscatine area most of her life. Her short stories reflect her love of family and nature. She also enjoys writing, painting and gardening. She is thankful to the Writers on the Avenue for the friendship, free workshops, supportive critiquing, and the opportunity to learn about and try new things.

G. Louis Heath (Ph.D., University of California at Berkeley, 1969) is Emeritus Professor of Ashford University in Clinton, Iowa. His books include *Leaves Of Maple: An Illinois State University Professor's Memoir of Seven Summers' Teaching in Canadian Universities, 1972-1978, Long Dark River Casino*, and *Redbird Prof: Poems Of A Normal U, 1969-1981*. He can be reached at gheathorov@gmail.com.

Madison Heisch just completed eighth grade at Rockridge Junior High.

Dustin Joy is an airline pilot and aspiring writer. He lives in western Illinois with his wife and three kids who love him very much but have thus far thwarted his dream of floating down the Mississippi on a raft.

Mark LeRette has been a Muscatine resident since 2005. He lives in West Hill district with his wife, Sharon, and two sons. He is a proud employee of MPW. He enjoys being involved in the community and serves on the Muscatine Historic Preservation Commission.

Salvatore Marici's poetry has appeared in *Toasted Cheese, Descant, Spillway, Penny Ante Feud, Prairie Gold: An Anthology of the American Heartland* and many others. He was the 2010 Midwest Writing Center Poet-in-Resident. He has a chapbook, *Mortals, Nature and their Spirits,* and two books, *Swish Swirl & Sniff* and *Fermentations* from Ice Cube Press. He served as a Peace Corps volunteer in Guatemala and is a retired agronomist.

Dennis Maulsby is a retired bank president living in Ames, Iowa, with his wife, Ruth, a retired legal secretary, and his dog, Charlie, a retired CIA operative. A son and grandson, Matt and Kaden, live in the Pacific Northwest. His poetry and short stories have appeared in *Lyrical Iowa, The North*

American Review, Haiku Journal, Spillway, The Hawai'i Pacific Review, The Briarcliff Review, and numerous other journals.

Ralph Montrone lives in Burlington, IA, and is a member of the Society of Great River Poets.

Dan Moore lives in Davenport, IA, where he is at work on an epic poem and a novel of naval suspense.

A graphic artist and cartoonist, Daniel Roberts' artwork has appeared in magazines and publications as well as a continuing comic strip named *Haley's Comment* that appears in the newspaper "Toons." He has written and illustrated four cartoon books. He has also written and illustrated a number of children's picture books, including the *Harrison and his Dinosaur Robot* series and *There's a Cookie Stuck to my Nose,* easy-reader chapter books including *Boy and Dinosaur, The Two Witches* and *Douglas Diggly, Super Spy* and the *Pep Squad Mysteries* series for young readers.

Denise Smith has lived in the country for most of her life. Nature is a wonderful teacher and is reflected in her writing. She has been a member of WOTA for 18 years and truly enjoys the camaraderie and support from the members.

Richard Thurston became interested in poetry while taking a poetry and music class in school. He likes the simplicity of Japanese styles of writing, namely haiku, cinquain, and tanka, that use highly descriptive words to create a picture in the mind of the reader. He is a machine operator at a plastic bottle making plant, and has two adult sons living in Muscatine and Wapello.

Misty Urban has published award-winning short fiction in several international journals and in two collections: *A Lesson in Manners,* winner of the Serena McDonald Kennedy award (Snake Nation Press, 2016), and *The Necessaries* (Paradisiac

Publishing, 2018). She is also a medieval scholar, editor, and essayist. She teaches at Muscatine Community College and runs femmeliterate, a website about feminism, literature, and women in/and/of books.

Clio Vogel wrote "The Month Poem" as part of an assignment for Mrs. Luna's first-grade class at McKinley Elementary in Muscatine. She enjoys writing and illustrating stories, playing with her pets, and riding her bike. She wants to be an airline pilot when she grows up. This is her first publication.

Rebecca Whitmore, a frequent volunteer with the local homeless shelter, wrote *Boots: At Home at MCSA,* about the cat that lives there. A copy is given to each child moving in to help ease their fears. She also published *Rusted From The Rain,* an anthology of poetry and stories written during a year of writing workshops with shelter residents. She is at work on a children's book of stories she and her grandson Clark dream up during their time together.

ABOUT WRITERS ON THE AVENUE

Writers on the Avenue is a nonprofit literary organization dedicated to promoting the literary arts in and around Muscatine, Iowa. WOTA has been supporting local authors since 1989.

Find out more about events, activities, and publications by visiting us on Facebook or at http://writersontheavenue.wordpress.com